Helen Orme is a successful author of fiction and non-fiction, particularly for reluctant and struggling readers. She has written over fifty books for Ransom Publishing.

Helen was a teacher for nearly thirty years. She worked as a Special Educational Needs Co-ordinator in a large comprehensive school, as an advisory teacher for IT and as teacher-in-charge for a pupil referral unit. These experiences have been invaluable in her writing.

Street**Wise**

Taking Responsibility

Helen Orme

Ransom

Street**Wise**

Taking Responsibility
by Helen Orme

Published by Ransom Publishing Ltd.
Radley House, 8 St. Cross Road, Winchester, Hampshire SO23 9HX, UK
www.ransom.co.uk

ISBN   978 184167 360 8
First published in 2014

CONTENTS

ONE

Problems at Home

'So why weren't you in school yesterday?'

'I've got a note from my mum.'

Leona pushed the envelope across the

desk.

Ms Prince, her form tutor, opened it

and read the note inside.

I kept Leona at home yesterday as she

had a heavy cold.

Yours sincerely

H Wilson (Mrs.)

Ms Prince looked suspiciously at

Leona.

'A heavy cold? You didn't have one on

Monday, and you don't have one now.'

'I got better last night.'

Ms Prince sent Leona off to her first

lesson.

She was worried about her. Leona had

missed a lot of school during the term,

and was falling behind with her work.

At break-time Ms Prince had a word

with Mrs Evans, head of Leona's year.

'It's not that Leona doesn't like school.

She's a bright girl and works hard in

class. But she's missed so many lessons

she's really going to struggle in her

exams.

'And then there's her homework.'

'What's the problem there?'

'It's often late, and very scrappy. It's

nowhere near as good as her work in

class.'

'Thanks, Greta. Sounds like problems

at home. I'll have a word with her.'

TWO

A Phone Call

Mrs Evans couldn't get much out of

Leona.

Whatever was wrong, she didn't want

to talk about it.

She decided to ring Leona's home and

talk to Mrs Wilson.

Later, she spoke to Ms Prince again.

'Now I'm really worried, Greta. I rang

Mrs Wilson, but I found it difficult to talk

to her. She kept telling me that everything

was fine, but her speech was really slurred.'

'Do you think she was drunk?'

'I don't know, but it sounded like that.'

'Do we need to get Social Services

involved?'

'Possibly, but I don't want to until we

are sure. I'll have a think.'

But before Mrs Evans had time to think

about it, something happened.

THREE

A Bump on the Head

The school nurse knocked on Mrs Evans'
door.

'It's Leona Wilson. She's had a fall in
P.E. It's not bad, but she's banged her
head and is feeling a bit sick. I think she

was tired and lost concentration.'

'What should we do?'

'I think she needs to go home. Shall we ring her mother and ask her to pick Leona up?'

Mrs Evans made a decision.

'No. I don't think Mrs Wilson can drive. I'll take her home.'

*****

Leona didn't want to be taken home,

but Mrs Evans didn't give her any choice.

When they got there, Leona got out of

the car and took out her key.

'I'll be fine. You don't have to stop.'

'Don't be silly, Leona. I've got to tell

your mum what happened.'

Mrs Evans pressed the doorbell.

FOUR

What's the Problem?

After a long wait, Mrs Evans heard the
sound of shuffling feet. The door opened
a few inches.

'Who is it?'

'It's Mrs Evans from Leona's school.

She's had an accident. Nothing serious,

but I've brought her home.'

The door opened.

'You'd better come in.'

Mrs Evans was expecting the house to

be run down and untidy, but it wasn't.

'Please sit down, Mrs Evans.'

'Would you like me to make some tea?'

Leona asked.

'Leona, you've had an accident! Go

upstairs and have a lie down. I want to

talk to Mrs Evans.'

Mrs Evans looked around. Next to Mrs

Wilson there was a table covered with

packets of pills.

'Thank you for phoning me about

Leona, Mrs Evans. I've made up my mind.

I need to talk. But it's so hard. I feel so

guilty about Leona.'

Mrs Wilson started to cry.

Mrs Evans leant over and gently held her hand.

'What's the problem, Mrs Wilson? How can I help?'

FIVE

Let Me Help You

'I have M.S., Mrs Evans. Multiple

sclerosis.

'I was diagnosed two years ago. At first

I could cope, but it's getting really

difficult, especially being a single parent.

23

It's the tiredness and the pain, you know.

'Leona is wonderful. She gets up early and gets things sorted. When she gets home she cooks a meal and does the housework.

'But I hadn't realised how it was affecting her school work.'

She started crying again.

'I won't tell Social Services. I'm so worried they'll take Leona away from me.

'Mrs Evans, what can I do?'

Just then the door opened and Leona

rushed in.

'I'm not going to leave Mum. I won't

let her down! Never, never!'

She hugged her mum fiercely and

glared at Mrs Evans.

Mrs Evans spoke softly.

'I should have guessed. Let me tell you

something. My daughter Catherine has

M.S. I know what it does, and I know the help that is available.

'No one will take Leona away, believe me. Will you let me help you?'

Then Leona did something she had never imagined doing.

She hugged a teacher.

Questions on the Story

◆ Why is Leona taking so much time off school?

◆ Why were Leona and her mum trying to hide what was happening?

◆ Mrs Evans made assumptions about Leona's mum. What were they?

Discussion
Points

◆ Leona hadn't told the school about what was happening at home. Why didn't she? Should she have done?

◆ Was Leona's mum right to depend on Leona in the way she did?

◆ How much should you help around the home?

Activities

◆ Write Leona's diary for the day.

◆ Research and write a report on M.S. (multiple sclerosis) and its effects on people.

◆ Design a notice for a doctor's surgery put up by a carer's support group, offering help and support.